PRIMARY SOURCES
OF
IMMIGRATION AND MIGRATION
★ IN AMERICA ★

THE IRISH POTATO FAMINE

Irish Immigrants Come to America
(1845–1850)

Jeremy Thornton

The Rosen Publishing Group's

PowerKids Press™

PRIMARY SOURCE

New York

For my brother, Timothy Thornton

Published in 2004 by The Rosen Publishing Group, Inc.
29 East 21st Street, New York, NY 10010

First Edition

Editor: Rachel O'Connor
Book Design: Emily Muschinske
Layout Design: Mike Donnellan

Photo Credits: Cover, title page, p. 8 (top) Trustees of the Watts Gallery, Compton, Surrey, UK/Bridgeman Art Library; cover and title page (left), pp. 12 (bottom), 16 (top, left), 19 (bottom) © Hulton/Archive/Getty Images; p. 4 Crawford Municipal Art Gallery, Cork, Ireland/Bridgeman Art Library; p. 7 (top) © Culver Pictures; p. 7 (bottom) © Jacqui Hurst/Corbis; pp. 8 (bottom), 15 (top) used with permission Views of the Famine website, http://vassun.vassar.edu/~sttaylor/FAMINE/; p. 11 (top) National Library of Ireland; p. 11 (bottom) Michael Nicholson/Corbis; p. 12 (top) New-York Historical Society, New York, USA/Bridgeman Art Library; p. 15 (left) Samuel B. Waugh, The Bay and Harbor of New York (detail), 1855, Museum of the City of New York, Gift of Mrs. Robert M. Littlejohn; p. 15 (right) Library of Congress Rare Book and Special Collections Division; p. 16 (right) © Corbis; p. 19 (top) Bandit's Roost, 39 ½ Mulberry Street, circa 1898, Museum of the City of New York, The Jacob A. Riis Collection; p. 20 (top) The John F. Kennedy Library/National Archives; p. 20 (left) © Bettmann/Corbis, p. 20 (right) Library of Congress Prints and Photographs Division.

Thornton, Jeremy, 1973–
The Irish potato famine : Irish immigrants come to America (1845–1850)
/ Jeremy Thornton.— 1st ed.
    v. cm. — (Primary sources of immigration and migration in America)
Includes bibliographical references and index.
Contents: Nineteenth-century immigrants — Life in Ireland — Famine strikes — Evictions — The coffin ships — Arriving in America — Life in America — Irish communities — Famous Irish Americans — Irish Americans today.
ISBN 0-8239-6831-6 (lib. bdg.) – ISBN 0-8239-8957-7 (pbk.)
1. Irish Americans—History—19th century—Juvenile literature. 2. Immigrants—United States—History—19th century—Juvenile literature. 3. Ireland—Emigration and immigration—History—19th century—Juvenile literature. 4. Ireland—History—Famine, 1845–1852—Juvenile literature. 5. United States—Emigration and immigration—History—19th century—Juvenile literature. [1. Irish Americans—History—19th century. 2. Immigrants—United States—History—19th century. 3. Ireland—Emigration and immigration—History—19th century. 4. Ireland—History—Famine, 1845–1852. 5. United States—Emigration and immigration—History—19th century.] I. Title. II. Series.
E184.I6 T48 2004
973'.049162—dc21
                              2003002302

Manufactured in the United States of America

Contents

Nineteenth-Century Immigrants

By the mid-1800s, America was in the midst of the Industrial Revolution. Steel mills, textile factories, and other industrial buildings appeared in cities throughout the country. Immigrants from all over the world, especially from Europe, came to America to find work and a better way of life.

One of the largest groups of people to immigrate during this time was the Irish. Between 1845 and 1850, Ireland suffered a terrible agricultural disaster when the potato crop was wiped out by blight. More than one million Irish died during the Potato Famine. About another one million left Ireland to escape starvation. Some went to Great Britain, but many left for America.

This painting by James Brenan (1837–1907) is called Letter from America. *It shows an Irish family in their cottage during the famine.*

Life in Ireland

Around the time of the Potato Famine, Ireland was under British rule. Most of the land in Ireland was owned by the British. Many of the landowners lived in Britain and hired landlords to manage their land in Ireland. Most of the Irish were poor and made their living as farmworkers. They rented small plots of land from the British landlords. They paid the high rents on this land by working for the British landowners. They had very little time to work on their own crops, so they grew a lot of potatoes, which were cheap and could grow with little farmwork. Potatoes were also healthful and could grow almost anywhere. The potato became the main source of food for the poor Irish.

Above: *This picture shows life in Ireland before the Potato Famine. A group of Irish people enjoy a good crop during harvesttime in Kilkenny.*

The Potato Famine, also known as the Great Hunger, started when a blight, spread by rain, wind, or insects, caused the potatoes to rot.

Left: *This painting shows a starving Irish family during the famine, in Carraroe, County Galway.*

Below: *This Illustrated London News picture shows one of the soup kitchens that the British opened in 1847 to give free food to the Irish.*

8

Famine Strikes

From 1845 to about 1850, most of the potato crop in Ireland was destroyed by blight. In 1847, the worst year of the famine, this disease destroyed 90 percent of the potato crop. Potatoes were the main source of food for the Irish. With no potatoes to eat, many Irish people starved. Prices for other foods went up because of the potato shortage, and the poor could not afford to buy the food.

At first, the British government provided some food and jobs to those hit hardest by the famine. They began a program through which Irish men were paid to build roads and buildings. The men were paid very little, however, and they had no time or money to plant crops.

The Irish Struggle

In early 1847, the British government organized soup kitchens to feed the hungry. However, the British did not want to continue to pay for this aid in Ireland. They closed the soup kitchens later that year. The government then passed a law that required soup kitchens to be paid for by Irish tax money. Most of the Irish were already struggling to buy food and to pay their high rents. They could not afford to pay the extra taxes as well. Thousands of Irish farmers and their families were evicted from their farms and homes because they could not pay their rent. Armed guards showed up to tell each family that they had to leave immediately.

Above: *This photograph shows an Irish family being evicted from their home by British police, during the famine.*

Left: *This is a picture of General George Charles Bingham. An English landlord on Irish estates, he was very much disliked by the Irish.*

Left: This nineteenth-century cartoon shows an Irishman, his belongings in a bundle, dreaming of a better life in America.

Below: Passengers are shown waiting to get on a ship bound for America at the Waterloo docks in Liverpool. Many Irish made the journey to America from this port in Liverpool, England.

The Coffin Ships

  The Potato Famine forced many people to leave Ireland. For most, the choice was either to leave or to stay and starve. The Irish had heard of opportunities in America, and many braved the seas to get there. So many people were leaving Ireland that many cargo ships were made into passenger ships. Conditions on the ships were terrible. Food and clean water were scarce, and disease was common. The ships became known as coffin ships because so many people died on the journey to America. The main ports of arrival were the cities of Boston, Philadelphia, New York, and Baltimore. Many Irish immigrants settled in the cities in which they arrived because they were too poor to move anywhere else.

Arriving in America

As soon as the Irish arrived at the port cities in America, it was clear that their new life was going to be hard. They were usually met by runners. Runners were people who tried to carry immigrants' bags and bring them to tenement housing in the city, charging high fees for the service. Tenements were buildings with many floors and with many families living on each level. Conditions were crowded and dirty. Many Irish had to beg on the streets. They were not welcomed in America. In fact, when advertisements were placed for jobs, they often ended with "No Irish Need Apply."

After a hard journey that usually took 60 days, the Irish arrived at ports such as this one in New York Harbor. This 1847 painting by Samuel B. Waugh is a classic scene of Irish immigrants arriving in New York.

Right: *This is a drawing of runners who waited to meet the immigrants arriving in America.*

NO IRISH NEED APPLY.

Written and sung by Miss KATHLEEN O'NEIL.

WANTED.—A smart active girl to do the general housework of a large family, one who can cook, clean plates, and get up fine linen, preferred.
N. B.—No Irish need apply. *London Times Newspaper, Feb. 1862.*

I'm a simple Irish girl, and I'm looking for a place,
I've felt the grip of poverty, but sure that's no disgrace,
'Twill be long before I get one, tho' indeed it's hard I try,
For I read in each advertisement, "No Irish need apply."
Alas! for my poor country, which I never will deny,
How they insult us when they write, "No Irish need apply."

Now I wonder what's the reason that the fortune-favored few,
Should throw on us that dirty slur, and treat us as they do,
Sure they all know Paddy's heart is warm, and willing is his hand,
They rule us, yet we may not earn a living in their land,
O, to their sister country, how can they bread deny,
By sending forth this cruel line, "No Irish need apply."

Sure I did not do the like when they anchor'd on our shore,
For Irish hospitality there's no need to deplore,
And every door is open to the weary stranger still,
Pat would give his last Potato, yes, and give it with a will,
Nor whisky, which he prises so, in any case deny,
Then wherefore do they always write, "No Irish need apply."

Now what have they against us, sure the world knows Paddy's brave,
For he's helped to fight their battles, both on land and on the wave,
At the storming of Sebastopol, and beneath an Indian sky,
Pat raised his head, for their General said, "All Irish might apply."
Do you mind Lieutenant Massy, when he raised the battle cry?
Then are they not ashamed to write, "No Irish need apply?"

Then they can't deny us genius, with "Sheridan"—"Tom Moore?"
The late lamented "Catharine Hays," and Sam Lover to the fore,—
Altho' they may laugh at our "Bulls," they cannot but admit,
That Pat is always sensible and has a ready wit,—
And if they ask for Beauty, what can beat their nice black eye?
Then is it not a shame to write, "No Irish need apply?"

Och! the French must loudly crow to find we're slighted thus,
For they can ne'er forget the blow that was dealt by one of us,
If the Iron Duke of Wellington had never drawn his sword,
They might have had "Napoleon Sauce" with their beef, upon my word,
They think now of their hero, dead; his name will never die,
Where will they get another such if "No Irish need apply."

Ah! but now I'm in the land of the "Glorious and Free,"
And proud I am to own it, a country dear to me.
I can see by your kind faces, that you will not deny,
A place in your hearts for Kathleen, where "All Irish may apply."
Then long may the Union flourish, and ever may it be,
A pattern to the world, and the "Home of Liberty!"

Above: *This song, printed in the* London Times *in February 1862, although meant to be humorous, shows the discrimination that was practiced against the Irish.*

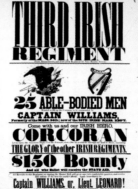

Above: When they first arrived during the 1850s, many Irish women were hired as maids in wealthy Americans' homes.

Left: Many Irish fought in the Civil War, which lasted from 1861 to 1865.

Life in America

During the 1850s, most of the Irish in America were very poor. In many cases this was because they had spent all their savings on the passage to America. They had few skills other than farming, and they usually ended up doing the jobs no one else would do. Most of the men found jobs as laborers, as construction workers, as deliverymen, or as ditch diggers. Many of the women worked as household servants. The Irish often lived in small basement apartments with no windows for natural light. Because of the poverty and terrible living conditions, about 80 percent of the babies born to the Irish immigrants living in New York City in the mid-1800s died.

This photograph, which was taken in 1882, shows a group of Irish clam diggers in Boston.

Irish Communities

The Americans looked upon the immigrants as a drain on society. The Irish were disliked by all, and they clung to each other for support. They did not give up under the pressure of hatred. Instead, they became stronger. Most Irish immigrants lived in communities where they could preserve their language and religion. As time went on, the Irish communities in the cities grew. Often, the Irish in America sent money to their families and friends in Ireland for the voyage to America. Over time, the Irish showed they were hardworking and fierce. They began to earn respect in America. Also, as other immigrants, such as the Jews and the Italians, began to come in large numbers, American hostility shifted from the Irish to the latest arrivals.

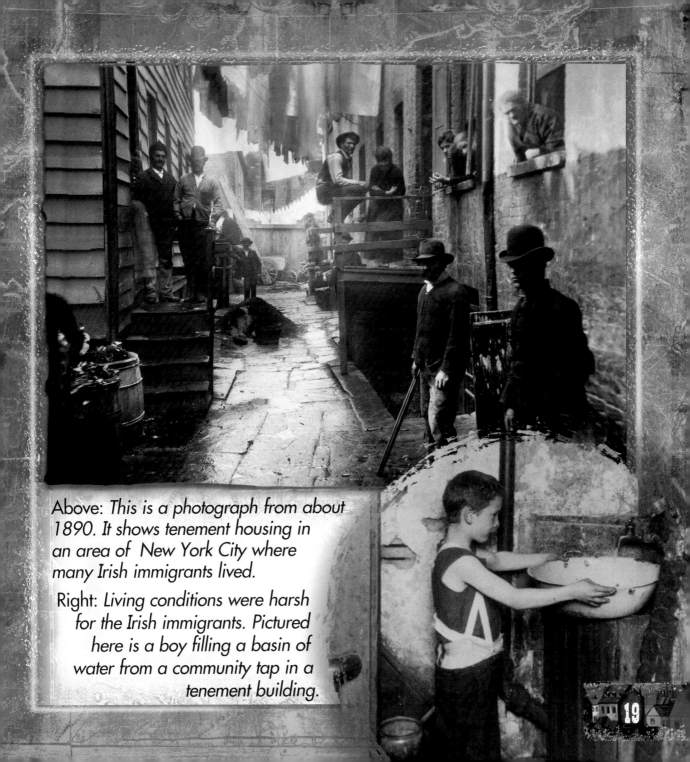

Above: *This is a photograph from about 1890. It shows tenement housing in an area of New York City where many Irish immigrants lived.*

Right: *Living conditions were harsh for the Irish immigrants. Pictured here is a boy filling a basin of water from a community tap in a tenement building.*

Right: John F. Kennedy was shot in Dallas, Texas, on November 22, 1963, when he was president of the United States.

Above: Irish American Nellie Bly created a great stir when, as a reporter, she traveled around the world in 72 days in 1889.

Famous Irish Americans

While many Irish dreamed of life in the "old sod," as they called Ireland, most knew that their lives and homes now were in America. Also, as time went on, they began to do better in America. There are many famous Americans of Irish descent. For example, boxing hero John L. Sullivan was born to Irish parents in Boston in 1858. Henry Ford, a pioneer in automobile manufacturing, came from an Irish family. Eugene O'Neill, a Pulitzer and Nobel Prize–winning author, was of Irish descent. John F. Kennedy was perhaps the most famous Irish American of all. Elected in 1960, he was the first Irish Catholic to become president of the United States.

Henry Ford, who founded the Ford Motor Company in 1903, is shown here in an early model automobile.

Irish Americans Today

When the Irish first immigrated to America during the Potato Famine, their migration was referred to as the American Wake. This was because the people leaving knew they would never see Ireland again.

Today in America there are more than 40 million Irish Americans. They are an important part of American society. People across the country celebrate St. Patrick's Day, an Irish holiday, by holding parades and wearing green clothing. The four-leaf clover, a symbol of Ireland, is seen as a good luck symbol. The Irish and Irish Americans have contributed to American music, literature, politics, drama, and many other areas of life.

Glossary

blight (BLYT) A sickness that kills plants.

cargo (KAR-goh) The load of goods carried by an airplane, a ship, or an automobile.

coffin (KAH-fin) A box that holds a dead body.

descent (dih-SENT) The line of family from which someone comes.

disaster (dih-ZAS-ter) An event that causes suffering or loss.

discrimination (dis-krih-mih-NAY-shun) Treating a person badly or unfairly just because he or she is different.

disease (duh-ZEEZ) Illness or sickness.

drain (DRAYN) Something that causes a lessening in amount, content, power, or value.

evicted (ih-VIKT-ed) Forced out of one's own home.

famine (FA-min) A shortage of food that causes people to go hungry.

immigrants (IH-muh-grints) People who move to a new country from another country.

industrial (in-DUS-tree-ul) Having to do with systems of work.

poverty (PAH-ver-tee) Being poor.

starvation (star-VAY-shun) To suffer or die from hunger.

symbol (SIM-bul) An object or a picture that stands for something else.

tenement (TEN-uh-ment) A building with many floors and with many families living on each level.

textile (TEK-styl) Woven fabric or cloth.

Index

Primary Sources

Cover. *The Irish Famine.* Oil on canvas by George Frederick Watts (1817–1904). **Inset.** Inscribed on the stone in the picture is "We are starving in Ireland," and the caption reads "The Herald of relief from America." Front cover of *Harper's Weekly*, February 28, 1888. **Page 4.** *Letter from America.* Oil on canvas by James Brenan (1837–1907). Crawford Municipal Art Gallery, Cork, Ireland. **Page 7. Top.** Harvest in Kilkenny. This engraving appeared in the *Illustrated London News.* October 30, 1852. **Page 8. Top.** See listing under Cover. **Bottom.** The central soup depot, Barrack-Street, Cork. Engraving by James Mahoney. From the *Illustrated London News*, March 13, 1847. **Page 11. Bottom.** General George Charles Bingham (1800–1888). Photograph by Michael Nicholson. **Page 12. Top.** *Outward Bound, The Quay of Dublin.* Engraving by T. H. Maguire in 1854 after a painting by J. Nicol. **Bottom.** *The Embarkation, Waterloo Docks, Liverpool.* Passengers are waiting to embark on a ship at Waterloo Docks. Circa 1850. **Page 15. Top center.** *Runners of the Olden Time.* From *Harper's Weekly*, June 26, 1858. **Right.** This satirical song "No Irish Need Apply" appeared in the *London Times Newspaper,* February 1862. **Left.** *The Bay and Harbor of New York* by Samuel B. Waugh. A classic scene of Irish immigrants arriving in New York.1847. **Page 16. Top center.** A recruitment poster for the Third Irish Regiment, which was led by Brigadier General Michael Corcoran. 1862. **Left.** Photograph of a maid carrying a tray. Circa 1870. **Right.** Irish clam diggers on a wharf in Boston. Photograph, 1882. **Page 19. Top.** *Bandit's Roost.* Photograph by Jacob A. Riis. Circa 1890. **Bottom.** A boy fills a large washbasin with water from a community faucet in the corner of a tenement building. 1910. **Page 20. Left.** Photograph of Henry Ford seated in one of his automobiles made during the early 1900s. Circa 1920s. **Right.** Nellie Bly. Circa 1890.

Web Sites

Due to the changing nature of Internet links, PowerKids Press has developed an online list of Web sites related to the subject of this book. This site is updated regularly. Please use this link to access the list:
www.powerkidslinks.com/psima/pfamin/